ISBN 978-1-331-68381-0
PIBN 10221034

This book is a reproduction of an important historical work. Forgotten Books uses state-of-the-art technology to digitally reconstruct the work, preserving the original format whilst repairing imperfections present in the aged copy. In rare cases, an imperfection in the original, such as a blemish or missing page, may be replicated in our edition. We do, however, repair the vast majority of imperfections successfully; any imperfections that remain are intentionally left to preserve the state of such historical works.

A
LETTER

TO THE RIGHT HON.

THOMAS HARLEY, Esq;

LORD MAYOR OF THE

CITY of LONDON.

To which is added,

A Serious Expostulation with the LIVERY,

On their late Conduct, during the Election of the
FOUR CITY MEMBERS.

By an Alderman of LONDON.

——————— Pudet hæc opprobria Nobis
Et dici potuisse, & non potuisse refelli.
OVID,

LONDON:

Printed for W. BINGLEY, opposite Durham-Yard in the Strand.
MDCCLXVIII.
[Price One Shilling.]

ADVERTISEMENT.

The Author begs that the Reader (before he proceeds
to the perufal of the following pages) would, with his
pen, make the two following corrections.

Page 15. line 8. *for*, had voted, *read*, had not voted.
Page 30. line 25. *read*, Queen Anne.

A
LETTER

TO THE

Right Hon. THOMAS HARLEY, Efq;

MY·LORD!

PERMIT me, at one and the fame time, to congratulate your Lordfhip and the public: your Lordfhip on being re-elected one of the Reprefentatives of the City of London in the enfuing Parliament; the public on having, by that means, fecured fo *uncorrupt* a fenator, and

fo

fo *able* a legiflator. And I the rather, my Lord, felicitate you on the prefent occafion, as it is very well known, that, for fome time before the election came on, you had very little chance of obtaining that honour, which you have now happily acquired. That this was really the cafe, appears beyond the poffibility of a doubt, from the fteps which you took previous to the election. Letters were written by yourfelf, by your brother, by your relations, and by all your numerous creatures and dependants, to the Liverymen of London, befeeching them for G—d's fake, for your Lordfhip's fake, for the fake of your family, for the honour of the City; in a word, conjuring them by every motive, which fear and apprehenfion could fuggeft to your own mind, or which you imagined could excite pity and compaffion in the minds of others, to re-elect you

one

one of the four City-members. Nay, letters were written to almoſt every houſekeeper in London and Weſtminſter, intreating them to uſe their intereſt with their friends among the Livery, to ſupport you on the day of election.

Not thinking yourſelf ſecure even with theſe reſources, you had recourſe, it is ſaid, to the good offices of the M——y, who ſent their inſtructions to Mr. ————, one of the clerks of the Board of Ordinance, in the Tower, deſiring him to ſolicit, or rather to command (for the M—— always command) the Liverymen of London to re-elect their four former members. And yet, my Lord, with all theſe mighty preparations, you had well nigh miſſed of your aim. For, by what fatality it happened I know not; but ſo it was, that, on the day of election you could ſcarce

pro-

procure a majority of hands in your favour. Sir Robert Ladbroke indeed, Mr. Beckford, and Mr. Wilkes, had evidently a majority of hands: but it was a doubt with many, whether your Lordſhip or Mr. Patterſon had the greater ſhow of hands; or rather, indeed, it was no doubt: the general opinion was, that Mr. Patterſon had the greater. And yet ſome how, either by the favour of the ——— or by ſome other means, your Lordſhip was juſtled into the number of thoſe who were returned as Members of Parliament.

This, my Lord, was a very great favour, from whomever you received it, as it ſaved you the expence of the poll, which you know is conſiderable. It is true, that when once the poll began, your Lordſhip ſoon got the ſtart of moſt of the other candidates, and by hard puſhing, you kept the ground

you

you had gained, and at laſt was declared to be duly elected. But was the election, my Lord, abſolutely free? Can any election be ſaid to be ſo, where acceſs is denied to the friends of any of the candidates? And yet, my Lord, was not this the caſe on the laſt day of the poll, when, by your Lordſhip's orders, the gates of the hall were ſhut on the frivolous pretext of keeping out the mob, but in reality, to exclude the friends of the other candidates? Beſides, my Lord, can any election be ſaid to be free, where the M——y openly interpoſe in the conteſt? But have not the M——y interpoſed in the late election, in the moſt open and barefaced manner? May not Mr. —— letter to the Liverymen of London, be fairly conſidered as an expreſs injunction from the M——y, directing them what members they ſhould chooſe?

I am

I am not, for my own part, fufficiently acquainted with the law of
parliament, to fay, whether fuch an
interpofition be a fufficient ground for
voiding the election; though I believe
the parliament frequently has, efpecially
when the Miniftry had not a majority
on their fide, voided, many elections
for a lefs irregularity. But this I will
fay, that Mr. ——————— has been
guilty of a moft flagrant violation of
the laws of his country; a violation,
which expofes him, if the law takes
its courfe, to the forfeiture of his office,
or, at leaft, to the penalty of a fevere
fine. I imagine, however, that if he
were to be tried by your Lordfhip, he
would efcape more eafily than the rioters, who lately broke the lamps at the
Manfion-houfe. Mr. ———————, it is
true, has violated the moft facred laws
of his country; laws effential to the
welfare, and even to the very effence
of

of a free ſtate (for there is an expreſs
law, prohibiting perſons poſſeſſed of
certain offices under the Government,
from being elected members of parliament, or interfering in the election
of members). The rioters have only
committed a ſlight treſpaſs : but Mr.
————— has done you a favour;
the rioters have done you an injury :
the former has contributed to ſecure
your election ; the latter have ex-
preſſed their contempt of your perſon,
and their indignation at your conduct :
and, therefore, I ſuppoſe that, in paſ-
ſing ſentence upon them, you would
have ſome regard to the motive of
their actions: nay, perhaps you might
adopt for once the jeſuitical maxim, *that the end ſanctifies the means* ;
and in that caſe Mr. ————'s
crime would be converted into a me-
ritorious deed, and the ſlight offence

B of

of the rioters aggravated into a moſt atrocious crime.

Waving, however, the freedom of the election, which it is neither my buſineſs, nor my intention to conteſt; I have a few queſtions to put to your Lordſhip, to which I ſhould be glad to hear ſatisfactory anſwers. And firſt, my Lord, I muſt take the liberty of aſking you, what could be your reaſon for departing from the practice invariably obſerved at all former elections of members of parliament for the **City** of **London**, viz. that of the four candidates, returned by the common hall, joining their names in an addreſs to the Livery. Mr. Wilkes, it is certain, had as great a majority of hands as any of the candidates; nay indeed, he had the greateſt majority of any one of them. Your Lordſhip, it is well known, had the leaſt majority; and, as I ſaid above, it is even a queſtion,

tion, whether you had a majority at all.. It might, therefore have been expected, that a man in this predicament would have behaved with some modesty.

And yet, my Lord, if fame says true, and fame, though sometimes a liar, often says true, this strange and unexpected innovation was owing to your Lordship. Sir Robert Ladbroke, it is said, and Mr. Beckford proposed, that the four candidates returned by the common-hall, should, as usual, join their names in an address to the Livery. This proposal was rejected by your Lordship, with a petulance and peevishness ill suiting your character. What, my Lord, could be your motive for such conduct? Was it pride that prompted you? You are, it is true, a Lord's son, and a Lord's brother; nay, indeed, you are a Lord in your own proper person: but then

you

you fhould confider, that you are but a temporary Lord; and that, in fix months hence, you will be plain Thomas Harley, Efq; merchant in London.

Befides, Lord's fon, and Lord's brother as you are, and temporary Lord in your own proper perfon, it would, I imagine, have reflected no difgrace either upon you, or upon any Lord, in the kingdom, to have had his name joined in an addrefs with Mr. Wilkes. I fhould rather think, that in the prefent cafe, it would have been, if not an honour, at leaft an advantage. A little of Mr. Wilkes's mercury mixed with the City lead, might have freed the metropolis from the opprobium, under which it has long laboured, of being the feat of dulnefs. But, perhaps, you was afraid, that the wicked wag would have made you the object of his wit, and the butt of his fatire; and as you

was

was probably confcious of having fomething ridiculous about you, you did
not think it prudent to have, for an
affociate, a man, who was fo perfect an
adept in the management of thefe wea-
pons. So far, my Lord, I own you acted
wifely; for, not to pay Mr. Wilkes a
compliment, which he does not de-
ferve, I believe he is very little capable of withftanding temptations of this
nature. Had he ever fpared you, it
would not have been out of refpect to
your noble birth; it would have been
out of compaffion to your weak un-
derftanding.

But, I think I can find out a better
reafon than pride, and that is intereft.
I fay intereft, my Lord: your Lordfhip is a citizen and a merchant; and
as fuch muft know, that intereft is a
much more general and more powerful
motive of action than pride. But how
could intereft operate upon your Lordfhip?

fhip? Why thus : your brother has
a place at court, being one of the
Lords of the Bedchamber ; and you
yourfelf have a lucrative contract with
the Government : and you probably
was afraid, left, by feeming to favour
Mr. Wilkes, or even by feeming not
to oppofe him, you fhould at once
deprive your brother of his place, and
yourfelf of your contract. In this
again, I own, you acted very wifely ;
but did you act freely ? Did you act
with that fpirit of independance,
which becomes a Reprefentative of the
City of London ? On the contrary,
could the meaneft member for the
meaneft borough in Cornwall have
acted more fervilily ?

But perhaps you have another reafon : you burned, when Sheriff, number 45 of the North Briton, and you
might think it beneath you to join
your name in an addrefs with a man,
whofe

whose writings you had committed to
the flames. I will allow you, my Lord,
to assume these airs, when your Lordship is capable of composing such a
paper.

Aye ! but you'll say, not only were
Mr. Wilkes's writings committed to
the flames : his person was also committed to the Tower. It was, my
Lord, and perhaps lodged in the same
room where once was lodged the person
of your grandfather. But Mr. Wilkes
continued in the Tower but a few days:
your grandfather continued there almost
two years. And as the time of their im-
prisonment was very different, so also
was the cause of their commitment.
Your grandfather was committed for his
treasonable attempts to defeat the pro-
testant succession, and bring in a po-
pish pretender : Mr. Wilkes was committed—I do not know for what—
but most certainly not for treading in
the

the footfteps of your grandfather. On
the contrary, his zealous attachment to
the auguft family now upon the throne,
and his rooted averfion to the flavifh
and enflaving family, which formerly
poffeffed, and was juftly deprived of it,
have always been univerfally known
and acknowledged. And indeed it is
not unlikely, that the too open pro-
feffion of thefe principles may have
drawn upon him the refentment of your
Lordfhip; efpecially if your Lordfhip
inherits the principles of your family,
which, in truth, is not improbable;
for bad principles, we know, like fome
kinds of difeafes, often run in the blood.

But if this, my Lord, was your motive, you will, I dare fay, keep it a fecret; and perhaps will alledge, as a more
plaufible reafon, that you did not
choofe to join your name in an addrefs
with a man of fo vicious a life, and fo

pro-

profligate a character. Aye, my Lord, was that really your reafon? was you afraid, left your own *pure, fpotlefs, fnow-white* character fhould have been con-tamminated by the mere circumftance of having your name joined in an ad-drefs with Mr. Wilkes? why truly, my Lord, if that was the cafe, you muft be extremely delicate indeed. But what, my Lord, have you to object to Mr. Wilkes's private character? Dare you fay, that he is not a man of honour, of honefty, and integrity? I would not advife you to fay fo, left the law fhould oblige you to unfay it.

But, perhaps, you will tell me, Mr. Wilkes is a man of pleafure: I admit it my Lord, Mr. Wilkes is, or rather has been a man of pleafure; and what then? Are there no men of pleafure in the city, and ftill more at court? Banifh all men of pleafure from London and Weft-minfter, and I'm afraid you'll make a

C * terrible

terrible gap indeed. Befides, my Lord, Mr. Wilkes will naturally be cured of this foible, as he advances in years; and, to fpeak truth, I believe he is in a great meafure, if not entirely, cured of it already. Let me likewife obferve, that man of pleafure as he may have been, he never did, fo far as I ever heard, invade, either by force or by fraud, the honour of any maid or matron : fo that even his pleafures have been regulated by the ftricteft maxims of honour.

In plain Englifh, Mr. Wilkes's great fault is, not that he is a man of plea-fure, but that he is not a man of prudence, or rather of cunning; and never endeavoured to conceal his foibles. Many, my Lord, of you wife citizens, often appear better than you are : Mr. Wilkes, I'm afraid, has fometimes appeared worfe. Had he been endued with a little of that gravity, which is fo common among the Citizens

of

of London, and of which, it muſt be owned, they have enough, and to ſpare, he might now have paſſed for as *pious*, as *ſober*, and as *continent* a man, as any that lives between Temple-Bar and Aldgate. But, fool that he was, he could never bring himſelf to put on the *maſk of hypocriſy*, which, like the *virtue of charity*, covers a *multitude of ſins*. Conſcious of being poſſeſſed of real virtues and abilities, he has ever been little anxious to acquire fictitious ones; and ſatisfied with the ſubſtance, he has never minded the ſhadow. He could never perſuade himſelf to aſſume that formal, ſolemn, demure air, which he well knew to be often a cover for vice, and almoſt always a cover for ſtupidity.

What's the bent brow, or neck in thought reclin'd?
The *body's wiſdom*, to conceal the *mind*.
I ſee the *fool*, when I behold the *ſcreen* :
For 'tis the wiſe man's intereſt to be ſeen.
And be this truth eternal ne'er forgot,
Solemnity's a cover for a ſot.　　　　Young.

Thus

Thus, my Lord, have I endeavoured to expofe the futility of all the excufes I ever heard made, for your refufing to join your name in the fame addrefs with Mr. Wilkes. But, whatever was your motive for this ftrange conduct, I will take the freedom of whifpering a fecret in your Lordfhip's ear, and it is this; that the name of John Wilkes, Efq; will be remembered and refpected by the friends of liberty, when that of Thomas Harley, Efq; is buried in oblivion.

A ferious

A serious expostulation with the Liverymen of London, on their late conduct during the Election of the four City-Members for the ensuing Parliament.

Gentlemen and Fellow-Citizens!

FOR I shall still distinguish you by those names; though I must frankly confess, I begin to entertain some doubt whether you have any just pretensions to the former; and for my own part, if your conduct on all future occasions be of a piece with that which you observed in the late memorable contest, I shall be ashamed to address you by the latter.

For what, let me ask you, can be more inconsistent with the character of a gentleman, than to falsify one's word, to break ones promise, to say one thing and do another, to inspire a man with the most sanguine hopes of success at the very moment you intend to disappoint him? If this be

C   acting

acting the part of a gentleman, then I have
formed a very improper notion of that character. But is not this the very part you
have acted towards one of your late candidates? Had not Mr. Wilkes, on the day of
election, by far the greatest show of hands,
of any of those who were put in nomi-
nation? But what sincerity there was in
these expressions of your zeal, the poll,
which is now finished, sufficiently demon-
strates.

The truth is, gentlemen, you will hold
up you hands for your liberties; you will
huzza for your liberties; you will rail, you
will bawl, you will clamour for your liberties; but I am fully convinced in my own
mind, that not one in six of you would
part with a single customer for your liberties. Aye, gentlemen, here is the rub:
you will do every thing for your liberties
that does not interfere with your interest;
but where that is concerned, you beg to be
excused: your little, partial, self-interests
must first be consulted, and then you will
afterwards take care of your liberties, if you
conveniently can.

Your

Your votes are given, not from any real regard to the merit of the different candidates, but merely in confequence of your connections in trade. For had you been actuated by the former of thefe motives, you could not have failed of giving your votes to a man, who, notwithftanding all that has been faid to the contrary by fome court-fycophants, has, I will venture to fay, done and fuffered more for the caufe of liberty, than any other man fince the days of the immortal Hampden. And is this the way to encourage others to ftand up in defence of your liberties, to neglect the man who has ftood up in their defence with fuch undaunted refolution ?

The real patriot, it is true, feels an inexpreffible pleafure in performing acts beneficial to his country, independant of all confideration in what manner they may be received by his fellow-citizens ; and in this fenfe furely, if in any, virtue is its own reward. But the fecret pleafure attending the performance of patriotic actions, is not a fufficient incitement to the generality of mankind : they want fomething more ; they

want

want the applaufe of their fellow-citizens;
not, I mean, that empty applaufe, which confifts merely in noify acclamation; for that,
it muft be owned, you have beftowed upon
Mr. Wilkes in as liberal and generous a
manner as ever you beftowed it upon any
perfon whatever: but I mean that fincere
applaufe, which proceeds from the heart,
which is productive of real and vifible effects,
and is followed by folid and fubftantial
favours.

And here, gentlemen, I'm afraid, you
will find it extremely difficult to juftify your
conduct. Upon the day of election, you
held up your hands in favour of Mr. Wilkes;
that is, you *virtually* promifed him your
votes, and *actually* chofe him one of your
reprefentatives in parliament. And yet,
when the neceffity of a poll appeared, and
you came, in good earneft, to give your votes,
you fhamefully turned tail, and left him in
the lurch. Upon what principles of juftice,
of equity, of honour, or of common honefty, fuch proceedings can be defended,
I am really at a lofs to determine.

And

And yet, gentlemen, I fhould be extremely glad to fee fome feafible apology made in your behalf. For I am equally afhamed and vexed to hear the greateft part of the Liverymen of London ftigmatized (as I daily hear them ftigmatized) as a parcel of *low, venal, and mercenary wretches*; or what is yet worfe, of *falfe and deceitful hypocrites.* I know it has been faid in your defence, that the common-hall, on the day of election, was filled with the mob, and not with Liverymen. But this I can affirm, upon the beft authority, to be an abfolute falfhood: nine tenths, at leaft, of the affembly were Liverymen; and they all of them, almoft to a man, held up their hands in favour of Mr. Wilkes.

The truth is, gentlemen, I believe moft of you have a real regard for Mr. Wilkes, but you were afraid to exprefs it, left you fhould offend your cuftomers; and as you thought you would not be diftinguifhed in the croud, you there gave full fcope to the natural fentiments of your hearts, and huzzaed and held up your hands for your favourite

vourite candidate. But the moment you came forward to poll, the piercing eye and inquifitive look of alderman fuch a one, 'fquire fuch a one, and Mr. fuch a one, who bought their bread from one of you, their meat from another, their candles from a third, and their foap from a fourth; I fay, gentlemen, the piercing eye and inquifitive look of thefe worthy cuftomers, ftruck a damp upon your mind, made you give the lie to your heart, and induced you, I had almoft faid compelled you, to withhold your votes from the man, whom, in your confcience, you preferred to all the other candidates. Such is the *independence, the boafted independence,* of the *worthy* Liverymen of the City of London!

Befides, gentlemen, you very prudently, I will not fay very nobly, confidered, that *Verba volant, fed litera fcripta manet:* I beg pardon, gentlemen, for quoting this fcrap of Latin : your *little Billies and Dickies,* if they have got into their *accidence,* will explain it to you. You wifely reflected, that as in polling you muft fet down your name in a book, which was open to

the

the infpection of all the candidates, that book (like the book of doomfday) would rife up in judgment againft you: that the feveral candidates would there have an opportunity of diftinguifhing their friends from their foes, and would certainly withdraw their cuftom and favours from thofe who had voted for them. And as to the promife, I mean the *virtual* promife, you had given to Mr. Wilkes (for fuch I muft confider your holding up your hands in his favour) I fay, gentlemen, as to that promife, you probably thought there could be no great harm in breaking it, agreeable to the maxim of the celebrated Thrafher and Poet, Stephen Duck, who fays,

If words are wind, as fome allow,

No promifes can bind;

Since *breaking* of the ftrictefft vow,

Is only *breaking wind*.

But, gentlemen, not only have you given your votes without any real regard to the merit of the different candidates, and merely

in

in confequence of your connections in trade, that is, from the loweft and moft mercenary motives; what is worfe, if I am rightly informed, fome of you have even fold your votes, and many of you kept back your votes to the very laft, in expectation that their price would ftill rife; nay, it is confidently reported, that votes were bought and fold as currently, tho' not as openly, as India-bonds or Bank-bills in Change-alley. If this be true, gentlemen, what is become of your wonted *probity and patriotifm?* How can you be faid to be fuperior to all *venality* and *corruption?* and in what refpects is the City of London preferable to the meaneft and moft defpicable Borough in the kingdom?

We have long heard of the *rotten parts* of the conftitution, and the neceffity of cutting off thofe corrupted members, in order to prevent the infection from fpreading: but if the accufation brought againft you by your enemies be well founded, the metropolis itfelf is the moft *rotten part* of the conftitution, and the ftate, of confequence, is

irretriev-

irretrievably ruined. For though a man may live with the lofs of a hand, an arm, or a leg, I never yet heard of any one that lived after having loft his head or his heart.

It was, therefore, very well obferved by one of your brother liverymen, in an ad-drefs he made to the public, " That if the " venality and corruption, which have been " long openly preying upon the limbs of " our country, have at laft fecretly feized on " her heart and vitals in the city of Lon-" don, mortifying is our condition! Let " fhame (fays he) for ever feal up our lips, " and the name of LIBERTY be heard in " our ftreets no more." Aye, gentlemen! but you may tell him, that if we do not hear of LIBERTY we fhall hear of Mo-NEY, and that is as good or better:

——— *quærenda pecunia primum;*
Virtus poft nummos ———

That is, gentlemen (left your *little Billies and Dickies* fhould not be able to explain it) give me a *plum,* and a fig for *liberty.*

D

The truth is, gentlemen, your *money* is your idol, your god: to that you will sacrifice your liberty, your religion, your honour, your conscience: in a word, every thing but ———— your *money*. And yet, gentlemen, let me tell you, that the inordinate love of money may defeat its own end; and that, from too eager a desire of acquiring, you may, at last, lose the means of preserving: for if once your liberty is sacrificed to your love of money, it will then be in the power of an arbitrary court to impose upon you whatever taxes, and levy upon you whatever contributions it pleases; and then you will find your money, your *dear*, your *beloved*, your *adored money*, slipping through your fingers you know not how, or perhaps ravished from you, whether you will or not. Think of this, gentlemen! and be content with possessing a little less money, in order to have the means of securing what you have got.

I come now to consider the objections, which you have to Mr. Wilkes, and which

you

you alledged in excufe for not chufing him one of your reprefentatives in parliament. And firft, fome of you had the weaknefs to fay, that you looked upon his offering himfelf a candidate for London, as an infult offered to the city.

But how, in G—d's name, will you prove it an infult? Mr. Wilkes is a gentleman by birth and education. He has already diftinguifhed himfelf in the Britifh fenate, more, moft certainly, than any of your prefent members; more, perhaps, than any member you ever had, Sir John Barnard excepted. He has fhewn himfelf, beyond any of his compatriots, to be a fteady friend to the rights and privileges of his fellow-fubjects. He has not only been a hero; he has almoft been a martyr in the glorious caufe of liberty. He has given repeated and inconteftible proofs of his being a man of ability, integrity, fortitude, and of every other quality, that can fit him for the difcharge of the important truft which he wifhed you to repofe in him.

How

How then can you call it an infult? what more would you have ? ——— O ho! gentlemen, I underftand you : you would have a man of fortune; a man poffeffed of one *plum*, or perhaps of two *plums*. Aye, aye, gentlemen, nothing, I find, but money will do in the city: money is the only paffport to all your favours. You have weighed Mr. Wilkes in the balance, and have found him wanting ——— in this moft effential of all qualifications. The city would be debafed in being reprefented by a man of fmall fortune. And yet, gentlemen, it is the general opinion, that fome of your prefent members are not men of very large fortunes.

Befides, permit me to obferve, that Mr. Wilkes was born to, and was once actually poffeffed of, as good a fortune — I will not fay as fome of your *city dons*; for he was never, I believe, mafter of a whole *plum*, perhaps not even of half a *plum* ——— but of as good a fortune, as one half the members of the houfe of commons. And tho', partly by a concurrence of untoward circumftances, partly by his own indifcretion

and

and want of oeconomy — for I will not defend him in points, where, I am perſuaded, he would not defend himſelf. —— I ſay, though partly by a concurrence of untoward circumſtances, partly by his own indiſcretion and want of oeconomy, that fortune be conſiderably impaired, and almoſt ruined; yet is he in a fair way of having it re-eſtabliſhed upon ſuch a footing, as will enable him to act with as much freedom and independance as any member of the Britiſh legiſlature.

Let me likewiſe aſk you on this head, gentlemen, how you can have the preſumption to ſay, that a man who has been choſen by ſuch a great majority of the independant Freeholders of the county of Middleſex, has offered you an inſult in declaring himſelf a candidate for the city of London? Are thoſe *low, venal, and mercenary wretches, the Liverymen of London* — for ſuch, it is affirmed, you have plainly proved yourſelves, by your late baſe conduct. —— Are theſe wretches a more reſpectable body than the Freeholders of

Mid-

Middlefex? You cannot, you dare not fay it: if you fhould, you will only add to our pity for your ignorance, the contempt that is due to fuch intolerable vanity.

Another objection, which, as it is currently reported, you have to Mr. Wilkes, is, that he wrote a fmutty and obfcene book, intitled, an —— —— ——, and attacked the king's fpeech with an indecent freedom. But here, Gentlemen, I apprehend you are under a confiderable miftake. Mr. Wilkes did not write this book: it was written by the fon of a worthy Archbifhop of Canterbury, himfelf a diftinguifhed member of the houfe of commons. Mr. Wilkes is, indeed, faid to have printed this book: and what then? would you anathematize him merely on that account? I am afraid, Gentlemen, that by this method of procceeding you would anathematize one half of the writers and printers that ever exifted in England. I will not, however, undertake to vindicate Mr. Wilkes in this particular. I think it would have been much better, had he printed no fuch book, or given the world occafion to fufpect that he had printed

fuch

ſuch a book. Nay, I think it would have been much better, had no ſuch book been written or printed at all; for I muſt freely give my verdict againſt all kind of books, that have the leaſt tendency to debauch the minds or corrupt the morals of the people.

Here, however, I cannot help remarking, that many of your grave, formal gentlemen, who exclaim publicly againſt all books of obſcenity, are yet the firſt to purchaſe and read them privately; and I make no doubt but if all the libraries in town were examined, more books of that kind would be found in the libraries of your ſober, ſedate gentlemen, than in thoſe of the greateſt rakes and libertines. Far be it from me, gentlemen, to juſtify the conduct either of the one or of the other; but I own I cannot ſuppreſs my indignation, when I hear an old hypocritical Lecher, who, under the maſk of virtue and religion, indulges himſelf in the moſt criminal pleaſures, damning to perpetual infamy in this world, and perhaps to eternal puniſhments in the next,

the

the man who ventures to write or print a little obfcenity.

As to the other part of the accufation, viz. that Mr. Wilkes attacked the king's fpeech with an indecent freedom, it cannot be denied, that Mr. Wilkes did attack the king's fpeech; but he attacked it as the minifter's, not as the king's; and as fuch it ever has been, and ever ought to be confidered, at leaft in parliament. It has, I think, been always held as a maxim in the law, that the king can do no wrong; that is, in his public capacity, he can do nothing: in other words, he can do nothing without the advice of his fervants, who muft be refponfible for his conduct. The firft prince that ever attempted to overturn this falutary maxim, was that unhappy and infatuated fovereign, King Charles the Firft, who, when any thing was done wrong, pretended that it was done by himfelf, not by his fervants, and therefore could not be queftioned. The confequence of which doctrine was, that no minifter could be called to account for any treachery he had

been

been guilty of towards his country. The confequence of which doctrine, were it once generally received, would (I will venture to fay) be the total fubverfion of our free government, and the eftablifhment of an abfolute and defpotic monarchy. For the propofition, when drawn out in its proper form, will ftand thus : *The king can do no wrong; that is, nothing which the king does mufl be fuppofed to be wrong, or ought to be queftioned. But the king may do any thing, or every thing : therefore any kind, or every kind of wrong may be done, and yet cannot be queftioned.* Let thofe who are better fkilled than I am in the quirks of the law, or the fubtilties of logic, difprove this conclufion, if they can. For my own part, it appears to me to be as plain as any demonftration in Euclid.

I therefore repeat it; as the king can do no wrong, he can, in his public capacity, do nothing. He cannot even be fuppofed to compofe his fpeech to the parliament; that is, and ever has been, confidered as the fpeech of the minifter, and ought to be treated accordingly. I own, indeed, that

E

as it is delivered by the king, it ought, on
that account, to be treated with great de-
cency and refpect; as every thing moft certainly ought that is communicated by the
fovereign. I likewife acknowledge, that no
man is at liberty to fay, in writing or in con-
verfation, the fame things of the king's
fpeech as he may fay in parliament. And
here, if I miftake not, lay Mr. Wilkes's
error; for I can, by no means, call it a
crime. In the heat of altercation and the
hurry of compofition, he forgot this ne-
ceflary diftinction. He forgot, or at leaft
he acted as if he had forgot, that he could
not decently, and perhaps not even fafely,
ufe the fame freedom with the king's fpeech
without as within the walls of St. Stephen's
chapel. But furely for this overfight (and
at moft it was but an overfight) he has already fuffered a hundred times more than he
ought in juftice to have fuffered. It ought
alfo to be confidered, that as Mr. Wilkes
attacked the king's fpeech, not as the king's
but as the minifter's, the reflections he
made upon it, muft be fuppofed to be le-
velled, not at the king, but at the minifter.

And

And in truth, if all thofe, who have faid, that kings' fpeeches often contain many groundlefs affertions, were to be treated as libellers; I'm afraid that, inftead of one, ten thoufand libellers might be found in the kingdom; as I believe there have been very few fpeeches delivered from the throne for this century paft and upwards, that have not been accufed of containing the groffeft impofitions. They were not, therefore, the king's friends, they were his enemies, who perfuaded him to confider the reflections made upon his fpeech as a perfonal infult offered to his majefty. The infult, if there was any, was offered to the minifter, not to the king. But it has always been the cuftom of weak and worthlefs minifters to juftify their meafures by the fanction of the royal name, and to endeavour to fcreen themfelves from popular refentment, by taking fhelter behind the throne.

The throne, however, never was, and, I hope, never will be able to protect any wicked minifter from the juft indignation of the people. If it fhould, then farewell to

E 2   our

our liberties. All refpect, I own, is due to the royal authority, while it is employed to proper purpofes; but if ever it fhould be employed to purpofes, with which it can, *legally* and *conftitutionally*, have no concern, it ought to be entirely difregarded.

Such, we find, were the fentiments of that patriotic, and yet loyal nobleman, the Earl of Offory, in the reign of King Charles the Second, who, when an attempt was made upon his father's life by fome affaffins, fuppofed to be fuborned by the Duke of Buckingham, addreffed that nobleman, even in the king's prefence, to the following effect: "My lord, I know well, "that you are at the bottom of this late at-"tempt upon my father: but I give you "warning, if by any means he comes to a "violent end, I fhall not be at a lofs to "know the author: I fhall confider you "as the affaffin: I fhall treat you as fuch; "and wherever I meet you I fhall *piftol* "you, though you ftood behind the *king's* "*chair*; and I tell it you in his *majefty's* "*prefence*, that you may be fure I fhall not "fail of performance *."

* Carte's Ormond, vol. 2, p. 225.

A third

A third objection which you have to Mr.
Wilkes. (for I have likewife heard fome of
you make fuch an objection to him) is, that
he, endeavoured to inflame the inhabitants
of one part of the kingdom againft thofe
of the other, and to involve his country in
all the horrors and calamities of a civil war.
But this objection; after all the fpecious
things that have been faid in fupport of it,
is as ill founded as either of the pre-
ceding.

Mr. Wilkes, it is true, did attack the
Scottifh favourite with all that force of argument, all that flow of eloquence, all
that keennefs of wit, and all that poignancy
of fatire, of which he is fuch a confum-
mate mafter; but he attacked him as a favourite, not as a Scotchman; and if he endeavoured to render him more odious on account of his being a Scotchman, it was
chiefly owing to the Scots themfelves; not
indeed of the Scots in general, but of fuch
of them as were the immediate creatures
and dependants of the favourite; who, confcious of the weaknefs of their patron's
caufe, attempted artfully to confound it with
the

the caufe of his country: fo that every Scotchman (and, to their honour be it fpoken, many fuch there were) who would not defend, at all hazards, the conduct of the favourite, were branded, by his creatures, as enemies to their country.

Such, I fay, was the origin of confounding the caufe of the favourite with that of his country. The opinion was firft broached by knaves, and afterwards adopted by fools; and I will take upon me to affirm, that it was never adopted by any other. The fenfible part of the Scottifh nation were too wife ever to give into fuch a ridiculous notion. They nobly and gallantly faid, that if Lord B——— was guilty, he ought not to be protected, becaufe he was a Scotchman; nor if innocent, ought he to be condemned, becaufe he was a native of that country. But had Mr. Wilkes attacked the whole Scottifh nation, without pointing his fatire againft any particular perfon, he might eafily have produced precedents for fuch a conduct. Dean Swift acted this very part in the reign of Queen. *Ann*. He wrote a libel againft the whole Scot-

tifh

tifh nation, fraught with fuch malice and virulence, as inflamed to the higheft degree the inhabitants of that part of the ifland, and induced the government to offer a reward for difcovering the author. Yet Dean Swift then was, and ftill is confidered as a very worthy man; and why Mr. Wilkes fhould for the fame conduct (though of the fame conduct he has not been guilty) be branded as an incendiary, I cannot well difcern.

Far be it from me, however, to approve of fuch illiberal proceedings. I am, for my own part, a citizen of the world; and I entertain a moft fupreme contempt for every one that is not. I efteem a man of fenfe, I love a man of virtue, wherever I find him, and wherever born or bred, were it even in the highlands of Scotland, or in the wilds of Weftphalia; and I defpife a fool, and hate a knave, though born in the city of London, nay in St. James's palace. I muft therefore difapprove of all national reflections. They are always odious, becaufe they are unjuft. Men of parts and probity are to be found in all countries, and

per-

perhaps too, in a pretty equal degree in all countries.

I own, indeed, that different nations are distinguished by different peculiarities of humour and temper. The English, for instance, are steady and resolute; the Scots, fiery and impetuous; the Irish, rash and headstrong; the French, airy and volatile; the Spaniards, grave and solemn; and the Germans, heavy and phlegmatic. But still I insist, that in point of moral and intellectual qualities (by which last I mean not actual knowledge, but the capacity of attaining knowledge) all nations are nearly upon a level; and that no one nation has a better right than another to throw reflections upon the rest. I therefore repeat it, all national reflections are unjust. But if Mr. Wilkes did endeavour to render Lord B——— more odious on account of his being a Scotchman, he very probably thought he might justify his conduct by the example of all political writers, who seem, time out of mind, to have adopted it as a maxim, that every ad-

vantage

vantage may be fairly taken againſt an enemy? *Dolus an virtus: quis in hoſte requirit.*

But Mr. Wilkes attacked Lord B——
principally, not as a Scotchman, but as a
favourite; and in this he acted both a generous and a patriotic part. Favourites
ever have been, and ever will be odious,
eſpecially if they intrude themſelves into ·
the management of public affairs. I would
not, indeed, deprive a king of the privilege, which every common man enjoys, of
having a friend, or, if you will, a favourite: but if he has, let him confine him to
a private ſtation, and not exalt him into a
public one: let him, if he pleaſes, make
him his groom of the ſtole, or chamber-
lain, or ſteward of his houſhold; but let
him not appoint him ſecretary of ſtate, or
firſt lord of the treaſury. In other words,
let him make him one of his menial ſervants, but not one of the ſervants of the
public. Within the former ſphere, a favourite may be ſafe, perhaps he may even
be popular; in the latter ſphere he can
never be popular, perhaps he cannot even
be ſafe. And indeed I think it is not im-

F   probable,

probable, that had Lord B——— continued to this day groom of the ſtole, as he was at the time of his majeſty's acceſſion, he might now have been one of the moſt popular noblemen in England. Every act of generoſity, which the king performed, would have been aſcribed to his counſel and ſuggeſtion. Whereas by forcing himſelf into a public ſtation, he has borne the blame (whether juſtly or unjuſtly I pretend not to ſay) of moſt of the blunders which, for theſe ſeven years paſt, the miniſtry have committed.

This diſtinction between the menial ſervants of the king, and the ſervants of the public, ought ever to be carefully obſerved. A king may, of his own mere motion, and according to his good liking, appoint the former ; but he never can, at leaſt he never ought, to appoint the latter, but in compliance with the voice of the public. A knowledge of the ceremonies and punctilios of a court, and of the common œconomy of a houſhold, may qualify a man for the firſt ; but nothing but the moſt eminent parliamentary abilities can fit him for

the

the laſt. Former parliaments have been ſo ſenſible of the neceſſity of this diſtinction, that they have frequently attempted to reſume into their own hands the appointment of the ſervants of the public. And, indeed, perhaps, it would be well for the nation, were ſuch an improvement made in the Government. We ſhould not then hear of the public treaſure being committed to the care of a thoughtleſs hair-brained youth, who, but a few years ago, gamed away his own private fortune; and all too for no other reaſon, than becauſe he has the addreſs to pleaſe the favourite, or becauſe during his childhood he happened to be the K——'s play-fellow.

I ſaid, that favourites were ever odious; and for the truth of this aſſertion, the whole Engliſh hiſtory will be my voucher. Gaveſton and the Spencers, in the reign of King Edward II. The Earls of Oxford and Suffolk, in the reign of King Richard II. Carr, Earl of Somerſet, in the reign of King James I. and Villiers, Duke of Buckingham, in that of King Charles I. are thinking inſtances to this purpoſe. And

F 2

what

what is remarkable, moft of thefe favourites came to an untimely end, as did alfo
moft of the unhappy princes who had diftinguifhed them by their favour. Nor, indeed, in this is there any thing furprifing:
for as all thefe were weak princes (the
truth is, none but weak princes ever have
favourites) and as every man in an exalted
ftation is expofed to the greater danger, the
lefs he is qualified for the duties of his office,
we have no reafon to wonder, that thefe
princes and their favourites met with the
fate which finally befel them.

Another argument, which I have to urge
in Mr. Wilkes's behalf, on this head, is,
that if he attacked the Scottifh favourite,
he only treated him as he would have treated an Englifh one: he would have attacked an Englifh favourite with the fame fpirit
and vehemence. The Englifh have always
pulled down their own favourites; and fhall
not they be allowed to pull down a Scottifh
favourite? Shall a man, becaufe born on
the North fide of the Tweed, be fecured
from the effects of that popular odium,
which has been the unavoidable fate of all
favourites

favourites without exception? Forbid it, juſtice! forbid it, common ſenſe! If any of the Scots ſhould be ſo very fooliſh as to maintain ſuch an abſurdity, pull down them and the favourite along with them. But I will anſwer for the generality of the Scottiſh nation, that they have too much ſenſe to maintain ſuch an abſurdity; and I can further ſay, from my own knowledge, that Mr. Wilkes has ſome as ſteady friends, and Lord B——— ſome as determined enemies, among the Scots, as among the Engliſh: friends and enemies, not from prejudice, but from principle; not on account of the trifling conſideration of the place of a man's birth, or the nature of his private conduct, but from a firm perſuaſion, that the one is a friend, the other an enemy to the liberties of his country.

A fourth objection, which you have to Mr. Wilkes, is, that he is an outlaw, and, of conſequence, not capable of being choſen a member of parliament; but of this objection the whole Engliſh hiſtory is one continued refutation. Outlaws have frequently been choſen members of parliament, and

declared

declared too to be legally chofen by the parliament itfelf, the fole judge of the qualifi-
actions of its own members. But, perhaps,
you gentlemen of the Livery of London,
may think yourfelves wifer than the great
council of the nation; though I queftion
much if the latter will be very willing, at
leaft in this refpect, to fubfcribe to your
decifion. In the 22d year of Q. Elizabeth,
that is, in the year 1580, one Vaughan was
chofen a member of parliament; and tho'
an outlaw, he was allowed to take his feat in
the houfe. In the 35th year of the fame reign,
the Commons exprefsly voted, and efta-
blifhed it as a general rule, that a perfon
outlawed might be elected a member of
parliament. Some oppofition, it is true,
was made to this practice by the fucceeding
monarch. In the 2d year of K. James I. Sir
Francis Goodwin was chofen member for
the county of Bucks; and his return, as
ufual, was made into chancery. The
chancellor, pronouncing him an outlaw,
vacated his feat, and iffued writs for a new
election. Sir John Fortefcue was chofen in
his place by the county; but the firft act
of

of the houſe was to reverſe the chancellor's
ſentence, and reſtore Sir Francis to his ſeat.'

This affair gave occaſion to a violent diſ-
pute between the king and the commons;
and many vehement ſpeeches were made
upon it in the houſe. "By this courſe,"
ſaid a member, "the free elections of the
"counties is taken away; and none ſhall
"be choſen but ſuch as ſhall pleaſe the king
"and council. Let us, therefore, with
"fortitude, underſtanding, and ſincerity,
"ſeek to maintain our privilege. This
"cannot be conſtrued any attempt in us,
"but merely a maintenance of our com-
"mon rights, which our anceſtors have
"left us, and which it is juſt and fit for us
"to tranſmit to our poſterity." Another
ſaid; "This may be called a *quo warranto*
"to ſeize all our liberties." "A chan-
"cellor," added a third, "by this courſe
"may call a parliament, conſiſting of what
"perſons he pleaſes. Any ſuggeſtion, by
"any perſon, may be the cauſe of ſend-
"ing a new writ. It is come to this
"plain queſtion, whether the Chancery

or

" or Parliament ought to have autho-
" rity ?" *

This matter, however, is now settled beyond the poffibility of a doubt. The authority of the houfe in determining the le-
gality of elections is abfolute, fupreme, and
uncontroulable by any other power ; and
as the houfe has repeatedly declared, that
outlaws may be chofen members of parliament, it argues either the groffeft ignorance, or the moft barefaced impudence,
to affert the contrary.

A fifth objection which I have heard
fome of you make againft choofing Mr;
Wilkes one of your Reprefentatives in parliament, is, that you were afraid, left; by
fo doing, you fhould offend the king. I
am really glad, gentlemen, to fee fuch a
fpirit of loyalty prevail in the City. 'Tis
a noble plant; cherifh it by all means.
But remember, that loyalty is an attachment to the laws, not to the king ; and as
far as I underftand the laws, they exprefsly

* Journals, 30 March, 1604.

forbid

forbid either the king, or any of his minifters, to interfere, in the leaft, in the
election of members of parliament. Should
you once come to be influenced in this matter by their advice, or a regard to their humour, we may expect, in time, to fee the
four City-members nominated by the ———
like the barons of the Cinque-ports, or the
fixteen peers for Scotland.

Befides, gentlemen, it is paying the king
no compliment, to reprefent him as enter-
taining a perfonal antipathy to Mr. Wilkes.
The king fhould know no antipathy, but
what the law infpires. If Mr. Wilkes has
offended the law, let him fuffer the punifhment, which the law directs ; but let
not the king, who is the chief executor of
the law, add to the punifhment from any
private pique or animofity. I'm afraid,
therefore, gentlemen that, in this inftance,
inftead of paying the king a compliment,
you have offered him an infult. You have
degraded him from the rank of a fupreme
magiftrate, fuperior to all little, low par-
tialities, into that of a private man, full
of fpleen, paffion, and prejudice.

Thus, gentlemen, have I impartially confidered, and, I hope, effectually overturned all

against choosing Mr. Wilkes one of your Representatives in Parliament. And now let me ask you, how you can answer it, I do not say to your own conscience (for that, I know, has no other standard of right and wrong, than your own little, narrow, selfish interests) but to the world around you, that you refused choosing, as one of your Representatives, a man, who had distinguished himself so nobly in the cause of liberty. How do you think it will found, in the annals of Great Britain, that, in the year 1768, the Liverymen of London refused choosing this man, who, but a few days after, was chosen by the independent Freeholders of the County of Middlesex? That the former were actuated by the base motive of venality and corruption, and the still baser motive of fear and cowardice; and that the latter acted only from a sincere regard to the real interest and welfare of their country? Let the fact, however, found as it will, it will certainly be related by the faithful historian; and will transmit, with infamy, the name of the Liverymen of London to the latest posterity.

A LIST of PAMPHLETS printed for W. BINGLEY, oppofite Durham-Yard, in the Strand.

1. MEMOIRS of the Court of Portugal, and of the Adminiftration of the Count D Oeyras : Taken from a Series of Original Letters, written in French, 2s. 6d.

" This Pamphlet is full of fo many attrocious Facts committed, and daily committing, by this Minifter, that, compared to him, Sejanus was a Saint, Richlieu a Lambkin, Mazarine a Nathaniel, Wolfey a Hermit, and Buckingham a Socrates. The Performance merits the Attention of every Britifh Subject ; and even Men of Speculation may reap confiderable Advantages by perufing it." Crit. Rev.

" This is a Tranflation of a well written, and apparently juft, Deduction of the Affairs of Portugal, from Anecdotes which appear to be genuine; fhewing that the moft important Interefts of that diftracted Kingdom, both foreign and domeftic, have been many Years facrificed to the Ignorance, Ambition, and Tyranny of a Favourite. Thefe are Circumftances (among many other) which will render the Memoirs before us generally agreeable, efpecially to a People, who are never more delicioufly regaled, than upon a roafted Statefman " Monthly Rev.

" This Tract is fufficiently interefting to engage the perufal of every well-wifher to the Peace and Welfare of Kingdoms. It confifts of a fhort Narration of a Number of extraordinary Facts, refpecting the Conduct of the *Favourite Minifter* of the Court of Portugal . Facts, which muft excite in every loyal and humane Breaft, the utmoft Horror and Deteftation of a Minifter, fo exceedingly cruel, avaritious, and defpotic."
Political Regifter.

2. The Mufical Magazine ; or, Compleat Pocket Companion for the Year 1767. Confifting of Songs and Airs for the German Flute, Violin, Guittar, and Harpficord. By the moft eminent Mafters, Vol. I. Price 7s. 6d. bound and lettered.

As Mufic has, of late, become fo much and fo juftly the Object of Public Attention, this may be confidered as a very ufeful Compilation, as it contains moft of the good Songs and Airs that hove been fung at the Places of Public Amufement for fome Years paft.

3. An Anfwer to a Pamphlet, intitled, Thoughts on the Caufes and Confequences of the prefent high Price of Provifion. In a Letter addreffed to to S——e J——s, Efq; By a Gentleman of Cambridge, 6d.

This Anfwer contains, among a Variety of other curious Particulars, a Scheme for reducing the Salaries of all Places under the Government.

4. The Hiftory of a late infamous Adventure, between a great Man and a fair Citizen. In a Series of Letters from a Lady near St. James's, to her Friend in the Country, Price 1s.

This day is published, price 1s. dedicated to Charles Jenkinson, Esq;

AN INFALLIBLE

REMEDY

FOR THE

HIGH PRICES

OF

PROVISIONS.

TOGETHER WITH A

S C H E M E

For raising for the Use of Government TEN MILLIONS,

BY LAYING OPEN THE

T R A D E

TO THE

E A S T-I N D I E S;

Humbly recommended to the serious Consideration
of the Right Hon. the Lords of his Majesty's
Treasury.

Sanabilibus ægrotamur morbis. Seneca.

THE SECOND EDITION.

Printed for WILLIAM BINGLEY, opposite
Durham-Yard, in the Strand. 1768.

CPSIA information can be obtained
at www.ICGtesting.com
Printed in the USA
BVHW091400211118
533724BV00021B/569/P

9 781331 683810